SAVED, SINGLE & SATISFIED

(TRANSITIONAL FLAMES SINGLES GO THROUGH)
Romans 5:15

By

JOHNOLA THIRZA CHAMBERS, Ph.D.

1stBooks - rev. 11/29/00

SAVED,
SINGLE
&
SATISFIED

A SPECIAL DEDICATION

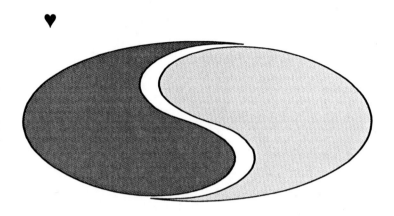

In the loving memory of Jonathan Millikens and David Harris, two Wonderful friends, who God called has called home for rest.

God allowed me to meet and have a friendship with two men who had biblical names and hearts of Gold. They both had a love for God and their families.

Jonathan and David had personalities similar to those of their biblical characters. It is not often that God allows you two meet two wonderful individuals, who knew the importance of letting go and letting God.

God had given them the wisdom at an early age, to know when the battle was not their own. They put their trust in God not in man. In this I will always remember them with the Love of the Lord.

I get great comfort in knowing, that for them to be absent in their mortal bodies is to be present with the Lord.

SPECIAL THANKS:

TO MY HEAVENLY FATHER THROUGH JESUS CHRIST, WHOM THROUGH ALL THINGS ARE MADE POSSIBLE.

TO MY MOTHER, ♥ MINETHA ISOLDA CHAMBERS, WHOM I LOVE AND HONOR FOR CONTINUING TO STICK WITH ME THROUGH THE FLAMES.

TO MY OLDER SISTERS AND BROTHERS, I LOVE YOU DEARLY. THANKS JUNE, JEFF, YOLANDA, AND YVONNE FOR BEING IN MY LIFE. YOU PROTECTED ME WHEN OTHERS WERE TRYING TO HARM ME. YOU TAUGHT YOUR LITTLE SISTER HOW TO LAUGH THROUGH THE PAIN. YOU HELPED ME STAY OUT OF TROUBLE WITH MOTHER.

FOR ALL YOUR HELP, LOVE, AND PROTECTION, THANK YOU.

TO ALL MY FRIENDS WHO DARED TO STICK AROUND DURING THE INTENSITY OF THE BRUSH FIRES, MAY THE LORD BLESS YOU FOR YOUR KINDNESS.

TO BISHOP AND PROPHETESS JOYNER, I THANK GOD FOR STRONG SPIRITUAL LEADERS WHO BELIEVE IN TEACHING THE WORD OF GOD. TO MY CHURCH FAMILY, REDEEM CHURCH OF GOD AND PROPHECY, THANK YOU FOR YOUR LOVE AND CONTINUED PRAYERS AS I WALK THROUGH THE FLAMES OF TRANSITION.

AGAIN, ALL PRAISES AND HONOR TO MY LORD, FRIEND, FATHER, PROVIDER, AND SAVIOR JESUS CHRIST.

SURVIVAL IN THE FLAMES

WHEN I SAW JESUS CHRIST.

I KNOW EVERYTHING WOULD BE ALRIGHT.

ALRIGHT.

HE IS MY EVERYTHING.

HE IS MY EVERY DELIGHT.

I WAS WALKING IN THE FIRE OF DARKNESS.

THERE WAS NO HELPING HAND.

PEOPLE LOOKED AND TURN THEIR HEADS.

AS THOU I WAS ALREADY DEAD.

THEN CAME A FIGURE OF A MAN.

OFFERING ME HIS RIGHT HAND.

I KNEW, I WOULD BE ALRIGHT.

FOR HIS COUNTENANCE WAS BEYOND
WHITE.

EVERYONE WAS ABLE TO SEE,
HOW MUCH LOVE AND MERCY HE
HAD FOR ME.
HIS EYES MET MINE WITH A FIERY
LIGHT.
THAT'S WHEN, I KNEW I WAS
ALRIGHT!

INTRODUCTION

"When thou passest through the waters, I will be with thee; and through the rivers, they shall not overflow thee: when thou walkest through the fire, thou shalt not be burned; neither shall the flame kindle upon thee. *Isaiah 43:2.*

This book is for all the single men and women trying to live in the here and now, without struggling every minute of every day. Often singles run through the different flames of life without any understanding of the importance of being single. Running from relationship to relationship, trying to find companionship has become the main focus. Therefore, they get burnt, trail after trail. We have run through situations before understanding the lesson God has prepared.

Therefore, we run around in a confused state, not knowing the way of escape. The flames of the experience are hot and painful. However, we never stop to ask the Flamemaker how to put out the flame.

Through this book, I pray that many will be delivered from feeling singleness is a curse. I pray that we understand that until we totally submit to God, and seek his Glory, a mate will not fill the void of loneliness.

Not that I speak in respect of want: for I have learned, in whatsoever state I am, therewith to be content. (Philippines 4:11)

CHAPTER ONE

WHO STARTED THE FIRE

Therefore being justified by faith, we have peace with God through our Lord Jesus Christ: By whom also we have access by faith into this grace wherein we stand, and rejoice I hope of glory of God.

And not only so, but we glory in tribulations also: knowing that tribulation worketh patience; And patience, experience, and experience, hope: And hope maketh us not ashamed because the love of God is shed abroad in our hearts by the Holy Ghost which is given unto us. (Romans 5:1-5)

We ask the question? Who started the fires in my life? You will have to take a self examination and determine the answer. We

1

know, God gives us the opportunity to make choices. He does not impose his will upon anyone. He desires that we submit to him and allow his spirit to take control of our thoughts and actions. However, many have not come to the full understanding of God's will and direction for them.

Therefore, I can only answer my question, "Who started the fires in my life?" The answer, "I started the fires in my life."

The Holy Bible is our instructional manual. Our leaders teach us how to follow the instructional manual but, we choose at times to follow our own manual. Therefore, during the season of test, we usually fail. We fail because we were not connected to hear God giving us direction. In order to be prepared for the fiery trails that so easily beset us, we have to be connected to the vine. We cannot be getting connected, we have to be connected. If you are straddling the fence when the trail comes upon you, then you will fall off the fence, and get hurt. " A double-minded man is unstable in all his ways." James 1:8

Double- minded people are always in a state of confusion. The decisions you make are usually made on poor judgment. Therefore, this decision will lead you seeking rest from God. One must understand, when the fiery trail comes upon you, if you are not under the blood and covenant with Jesus, then Satan will attack with all spiritual wickedness to destroy you. God does not want to destroy you. He allows the fiery trails to occur to strengthen your faith, hope and character.

In my case, God wanted me to have more spiritual depth and perseverance. He allowed me to make choices that would teach me some valuable lessons. The choices I made delayed my blessings. Get this straight my blessings were delayed not denied. I didn't understand why my plan to get married, have a strong ministry, and be prosperous in wealth and health was not coming to pass. However, one day when I was reading the Word of God, I read some powerful words. "Tribulation worketh patience, and patience, experience, and experience hope, and hope maketh not ashamed."

When I first read these words, I didn't get it. I read it again. My first thought was God is telling me, that I have to go through tribulation to get patience, and the patience I receive will help me deal with my experiences. (Past or Present). Through my experiences, I will have hope regardless of what the circumstances. It sounded good. However, I could not imagine in my finite mind, what current experiences would help me get through past child hood traumas. I just want you to know over the next several years of my life, God revealed the understanding of these scriptures. It has taken me 7 years to fully understand the importance of these scriptures. I am sharing my experiences with you, so you don't take the same route.

When I first accepted Jesus as my personal savior, I wanted to know all about him. Therefore, I would pray and fast. I would study my word. I would go to bible class, attend evangelistic services, Sunday school, and all day Sunday service. No one could tell me that I did not understood my Lord and Savior. *(mistake number one: we can't comprehend the mind of God. His ways are higher than our ways.   His thoughts are higher than our thoughts.)*

In any event, since I thought I had obtained all the knowledge I needed to know about the Lord, I wanted my husband! I wanted to get married! I had finished getting my Masters degree in Social Work.   I had a good supervisory job.   I was in good shape. Therefore, I was indeed ready for my husband. *(Don't laugh. I was still young in the Lord.)*

In lieu of all my accomplishments, I asked a friend who had recently married, about marriage.   She told me, even Inspite of my accomplishments, I needed to be prepared for marriage. She continued to say she didn't think I was ready for marriage. Well, needless to say, the spirit doesn't dwell with man always. So my first reaction was, she needs to shut up and go sit down.   Then, I thought, prepare for what?" She knew, that I had ordered Bride Magazines. My sisters would be the matrons of honor. The seven brides maids were wearing gold. My friend who lived in Boston, named Alesia, would sing a solo. My mother would make the wedding cake. My jr. brides maids would be my nieces. In fact, I had it all planned out except for the hall and the man. I admit the man is the most important factor to getting married, but I was working by faith.

In my haste, I did not realize that she wasn't talking about materialistic preparation. She was referring to the spiritual preparation needed for my marriage and family to succeed.

Every wise woman buildeth her house: but the foolish plucketh it down with her hands. Proverbs. 14:1

Who can find a virtuous women? For her price is far above rubies. The heart of her husband doth safely trust in her, so that he shall have no need of spoil. Proverbs 31:10-11

In order to build my house I needed more wisdom and knowledge. I needed to be detailed for this new position. Today, I understand a help-mate needs to know how to fast, pray, budget, and listen. The fruit of the spirit is love, joy, peace, long-suffering, gentleness, goodness, faith, meekness, and temperance. One should have the fruits of the Spirit totally operational to be married until death.

In viewing myself, I recognized that all the fruits of the spirit were not operational in my life. In fact some of my natural skills were not operational. I spent money when, where, and how I wanted. I had patience for who I wanted. I would pack up and go away when I wanted. My friends would often call me a spoiled brat.

However, I would say, " I just like things my way, and that is not spoiled. It is called Independence!"

Then it hit me like a brick off of a building. When I get married, I couldn't have things my way. I would have another opinion in the house. I would have a husband, whose opinion, I would be expected to reverence. I don't know if you could imagine the impact of this news. But, let's just say if I had to go to the bathroom, I'd be wet.

Are you are reading this saying, she is so dramatic. Well, you would be dramatic too, if your reality was nothing but a fantasy. I couldn't imagine making this ninety degree turn around. I asked God how, when, and who is going to help me make these drastic changes. I asked God this question over and over again?

However, he did not answer, so I prayed a different prayer.

I began to pray for more patience, peace, understanding, wisdom, knowledge, and spiritual discernment. Little did I know, in order to obtain patience and peace you have to go through the battle field. To obtain wisdom, you have to forget the ways of the world. You have to Place aside your will and way to embrace God's will and direction. To get knowledge you have to read and meditate on the word day and night. To receive patience, you have to be long-suffering. To learn how to be long-suffering, you have to go through many fiery trails.

My fiery trails came through my friends, family, job, finances and health. The trails did not come at once; like Job. Job had a <u>TEN ALARM FIRE!</u> He lost his children and stock in an evening. My fire started in one room and slowly moved throughout the house. The first year the trail of friends and finances came upon me. The second year finances and flesh. The third year finances, flesh, and family. The fourth year family, friends, and job. The fifth year flesh, finances, friends, health, and job. The six year health, health, health, and friends.

My patience for long-suffering was not active! Therefore, the same trails carried over year after year. My friends did not understand why I kept striving for perfection. My family trails were the average trails of a family. My health failed because my anchor wasn't totally in Jesus. I was still trying to operate out of the confinements of my head.

The fiery trails had me feeling trapped. I was choking from the fumes. I could not see God to the right or the left. I did not feel any release from the inside. I could not make it anymore on my own. It was when I collapsed in body and fainted in mind that the Lord ministered unto me.

When my soul fainted within me I remembered the Lord: and my prayer came in unto thee, into thine holy temple. Jonah 2:7

The Lord never wants us to collapse from our trails. However, if we continue to kick against the prick, then that is what happens. Our peace and rest will come when we come under the subjection of the Lord. Humble yourself under the mighty hand of the Lord, and ask for HELP!. The Lord's grace is sufficient for thee.

Humble yourselves therefore under the might hand of God, that he may exalt you in due time: Casting all your cares upon him, for he careth

12

for you. Be sober, be vigilant; because your adversary the devil, as a roaring lion, walketh about seeking whom he may devour: Whom resist steadfast in the faith, knowing that the same afflictions are accomplished in your brethren that are in the world. (I Peter 5:6-9)

It is Time to Pray, to ask Our Father to help you to Stop Kicking Against the Prick.

Heavenly Father, through your precious son Jesus:

Father, I thank you for your love and mercy. I acknowledge that I can do nothing without you. I need your help Father! You are the potter and I am the clay. I need you to help remold me Lord. I have been trying to do things my way. I have been trying to get a mate on my own terms. I have not really sought your council on waiting for a helpmate. I have been running in and out

13

of relationships, hoping one of them would be the one. I recognize now Father, that I cannot do things my way. I have to be under the guidance of your will and your way. Therefore, Father, I ask you to forgive me of my sins of omission and commissions. Forgive me of the times when I knew not to proceed in a relationship and proceeded anyway. Forgive me for not submitting to the Holy Ghost. Forgive me for being full of pride and self-righteous. I desire to be in your will and way. I desire to one day be married and have a family. However, most of all I desire that I be in accordance with your word. I want a helpmate who will be on one accord. I want us to walk together and agree as your word says. Therefore, Lord cleanse me of my sins. Wash me and give me a fresh anointing. Let me wait patiently on my helpmate. In the meantime, allow me to wait contentedly, working in the kingdom for your glory.

I praise you now father for the victory. I give you all the honor and glory. I love you and magnify for being a God of a second chance. This day _____, I commit my mind, spirit, and soul to you. Help me daily to crucify the flesh from the top of my head to the soul of my feet. Help me to watchful and prayerful, for I know my flesh is weak. Help me Lord to walk upright before you on a daily basis. Help me, keep my body under subjection. Help me to present my body a living sacrifice, Holy and acceptable unto, you which is my reasonable service.

I thank you for the fresh anointing. I praise for the Victory in your Name.

In Jesus Name, I pray Amen.

CHAPTER TWO

SEEKING PROTECTION
FROM THE FLAMES

I will lift up my eyes unto the hills, from whence cometh my help. My help cometh from the Lord, which made heaven and earth. He will not suffer thy foot to be moved; he that keepeth thee will not slumber. Behold, he that keepeth Israel shall neither slumber nor sleep. The Lord is thy keeper: the Lord is thy shade upon the right hand. The sun shall not smite thee by day nor the moon by night. The Lord shall preserve thee from all evil: he shall preserve thy soul. The Lord shall preserve thy going out and thy coming in from this time forth, and even for evermore. Psalms 121:1-8

Psalms 121, tell us when we are in trouble to look up to Jesus. Friends and Family should not be your main source for help. Don't misunderstand my statement. Family is very important. A good structure family, will help each other out in the time of trouble. However, there are trouble and woes that family and friends cannot help you. That is why our help cometh from the Lord.

Family, Friends, and other love ones can give temporal cares to your wounds. However, God can heal your broken heart, open a new financial door, cure your body of disease, and still allow you to have Joy through all the pain. No human has the power to handle all those situations at once and still tend to others. See God can take care of your heart aches, my heartaches, and the heartaches of all his people at the same time. He is omniscient, omnipresence, and omnipotent. He knows what you need, when you need, and how much you need.

Shadrach, Mechach, and Abendego, as an example of seeking protection from the flame. Although in their cases, they were seeking protection from real flames of fire. These three Hebrew boys, knew that their God could deliver from the fiery furnace. They knew that no man had the authority to saved them based on the decree of the law.

As singles, we are not facing flames of fire. However, some of you are burning like there are flames of fire. That is why it is very crucial, that you get under immediate subjection of the Holy Ghost. The devil desires to sift you as wheat. He does not just want you to fornicate. He wants you to fornicate, then lie about it. Then once you have done that, take you a little further, with drinking and whoremonging, and whatever else he can get you into. Sex is not the devils ultimate plan for you. His ultimate plan is death and destruction.

Some of you are already playing with dangerous situations. You better come out of them. Hell is real and so is AIDS, Venereal Diseases, and Pregnancy. The devil wants to mess up your testimony. His wants you to get caught with your pants down. Once you get caught with your pants down, he is going to tell your business to everyone. This is how the enemy works. He wants to make you ashamed and embarrassed. He wants you to go into isolation and then depression. However, I want you to know the devil is a liar. You will not be a slave to any sex demon. I rebuke that demon of lust, in the name of Jesus. You have the authority. Tell the devil to get off of you. Tell that Lust demon, by the power and blood of our savior Jesus Christ you command it to take flight back to the pit of hell where it came from. Tell yourself, I am a child of the King. I am more than a conqueror. I will keep my body Holy. I will not have sex without marriage. I am not a boy/girl toy for any unholy person. I WILL NOT HAVE SEX WITHOUT MARRIAGE.

You have to continue to rebuke the enemy on a daily basis to gain the strength you need to fight off the temptations that will come your way. You will have to continually affirm who you are in Christ, by reading your word. Last but not least, you must remember there will be times you will need refuge to be able to rest and regain the strength you need to stay focused.

There are discouraging times on this journey. It sometimes looks like God is not answering, your prayers. All you see are you friends getting married and having children. At times it seems like there aren't any prospects or even suspects to date. This is when you seek refuge from the Almighty, Jesus Christ.

He that dwelleth in the secret place of the most High shall abide under the shadow of the Almighty. I will say he is my refuge, my fortress, my God. In him will I put my trust. He shall cover thee with His wings, and under His wings shall I trust; His truth shall be my shield and buckler. Psalms 91:1-3

I had to first come to the realization, that there is no other help than God. The only Secret Place is that of the Most High. I sought refuge and help from friends and family and that was disastrous. My friends and family are great, however, they are not God. They too were seeking refuge and shelter from loneliness, depression, poverty, racism, sexism, etc. When I placed all my trust and faith in God, he provided the shelter and rest, I was so desperately seeking.

<u>God is my Refuge, my Fortress, and my God</u>. The bible tells me that since, God is the Almighty God on High, he has the ability to protect and shield me from any situation. There is no other god, like our God. Our God gave his only begotten Son, that we may live. He gives us shelter from the darkness of Hell. He gave me and my family food in the time of trouble. He healed me from sickness as a baby. He covered me through adolescent storms. He continues to shield me from the fiery darts of destruction.

In seeking protection from the flames, you have to trust the flamemaker. You have to know that God can, and he will protect. When it seems as thou there is no way of escape from a situation God will provide the way of escape.

During my many years of trails and tribulations, I never sought refuge. I would ask God to help me, but then I would just keep my same pace. I would go to work, school, home, and then church. I didn't stopped to hear the Lord tell me where I would find rest. I was preoccupied with my agenda of getting married, wealth, and success. Therefore, my agony prolonged.

We have to be careful of the behavior described above. When we have our own agenda, then the devil usually attacks. He knows we are not connected to the vine the way we should. The old man in me was trying to return. Don't miss understand, I was still attending church. However, it had become a formality. I wasn't entering into the building with thanksgiving in my heart. I was entering into the building, because it was expected.

For do I now persuade men or God? Or do I seek to please men? For if I yet pleased men, I should not be the servant of Christ. Galatians 1:10

The devil recognizes when our focus changes. He know my focused had changed. He knew, I had an agenda that I wanted to occur at this time. Therefore, he worked on my patience. I became short tempered with friends and family members. I remember thinking, "I pay my tithes and offering. I come to church regularly. I teach Sunday school. I am the Youth Pastor. Why am I not getting my blessings? What more could I do God?" God did not answer. This made me more discouraged. My Bishop would try to encourage me, but I would listen in doubt. I felt it was his job to encourage his flock. Therefore, I would come to church empty and leave empty. I figured maybe, God needed a little help. Maybe, I wasn't making it known to the appropriate individuals that I am single. How many of you know, God does not need any help? Well, I was on my way to finding out, God does not appreciate little gods; and that's what we are when we try to take over God's duties.

I attempted to help God, and made a big mess. I didn't have a clue to what I was doing. I changed hair styles, starting getting my nails wrapped, and working out. These things are not bad, if you are doing them for yourself. However, we all know by now, I was getting prepared to trap a man. Well, let's just say everything that took the bate, gave me more aggravation then I already had. Keeping my body under subjection and trying to date was not mixing. The brothers were impressed, but still trying to undress me. However, when God has a plan for your life, he makes a way of escape. I learned from those several years of dating, that I can't do it my way. My way left me feeling broken-hearted and alone. I realized being single and with God is better than feeling alone and married to the wrong man.

Can two walk together, except they be agreed? Amos 3:3 Sampson and Delilah is a wonderful illustration of Amos 3:3. Sampson could have had any woman from his own people, however, he allowed the enemy to trick him. Therefore, instead of being prayerful and waiting on God, he went and took a wife from the enemies camp. Sampson did not believe that beautiful Delilah could or would do him any harm. Well, you know the old saying, "not everything that looks good is good for you." When a person does not belleve in the fact that Jesus is God's only begotten son; then your conversation should only be about salvation. Don't play with fire, or you will get burnt. Rather than get burnt, put your trust in God, and wait on him.

In him will I put my trust. In God will I put my trust. In God will I put my trust. I repeated the sentence twice, because we have a tendency to put our trust in our paycheck, friends, family and ourselves. We are creatures of habit, therefore, we usually return to what we know when we are in crisis. So, in order to help us stay focused say to yourself :

I have to stay in God's will and direction. I have to wait upon the Lord. I know Jesus hears my cry. He promised, to give me the desires of my heart. When I am feeling lonely, I will pray. When I get discouraged, I will sing. When I can't sing or pray, then I will remember the promises of God. Because, I know, God will never leave me nor forsake me. He will give me a helpmeet that will be best for me. He will allow me to prosper in health and wealth; as my soul prosperth. He will save my unsaved love ones. I must always remember my blessings are in God's timing not mine.

He shall cover thee with His wings, and under His wings shall I trust; His truth shall be my shield and buckler.

Wings are soft and light, but they extend to carry the bird to its destination. God has been placing his wings over my life. When I was sick, and the doctors did not know what else to do, Jesus placed his wings over me an healed me. He gently carried me, since I could not carry myself. He ministered to my soul. He gave me rest from worry. He gave me hope to live. He loved me Inspite of my infirmity. He loved me even thou, it looked like I'd die.

There are not many people willing to sign up for the job that Jesus did for me during my sickness. Therefore, it is important that the spouse I receive be willing to love in sickness and health. God healed me completely. However, you don't want someone who will only be there when you are well and look good. You want someone who will love you when you are sick, gained extra pounds, and wrinkled.

I trust God will continue to be my shield and buckler. He has been there all the time, and I don't doubt he will continue to be there. Even when God gives you someone in your life. God is still your shield and buckler. Won't you lean on him today. Won't you acknowledge to our Savior that you need him as your shield and buckler. Jesus is the Highest Personal Body

Guard you can ever retain. He is the only Personal Body Guard, that will never need a break to sleep, eat, or go to the bathroom. He will never leave you, nor forsake you. Jesus will never give you more than you can bare. He has his angels encamped around you. He will give you that peace that surpassess all understanding. He will gently put a song of praise in your heart, as he rocks you to sleep. Isn't it nice to be under the watch-care of Jesus Christ.

Let us Pray:

Heavenly Father In Your Son's Name Jesus:

O, Lord, I will praise you for the protection you have given me over the years. God you are my salvation. I will put my trust in you, and I am not afraid, for I know you are the Lord Jehovah. You are my strength and my fortress. I will sing praises unto you Lord. Continue to help me dwell in the secret place under you. Help me not to go astray and seek refuge from other sources.

I know you are my only strong tower. I thank you for encamping your angels around me daily for protection from hurt, harm, and destruction. I thank you for interceding on my half to the Father. I thank you for loving me. I thank you for dying for me on Calvary. I know that you love me, for you have come into a life of sin and continually try to help me live a life of holiness. I thank you for caring about me. I love you Lord.

In Jesus Name, I pray

Amen

CHAPTER THREE

WATER ON THE FIRE

Remember ye not the former things neither consider the things old. (Isaiah 43:18)

It is dangerous to sit around thinking about things in the past. The devil has you thinking about past relationships. When you live in the past, you leave room for the devil to come in and play with your mind. (STOP PLAYING WITH DEAD THINGS.)

When the unclean spirit is gone out of man, he walketh through dry places, seeking rest, and findeth none. Then he saith, I will return into my house from whence I came out, and when he is come, he findeth it empty, swept, and garnished. (Matthew 12:43-44)

The enemy will try to oppress you with feelings of loneliness, hopelessness, and depression. He will continue to play with your emotions until you lose faith. No faith, No deliverance, because it is impossible to please God without faith.

Behold, I will do a new thing: now it shall spring forth, shall ye not know it? I will make a way in the wilderness, and rivers in the desert. (Isaiah 43:19)

There will be point in your life, when trails will make you feel isolated. You will feel like God has left you in the desert, without food, water, or a directional map.

It is possible to live without the map and the food. However, it is impossible to live without water. How do you get to the living waters of God? The answer, is through faith.

NOW faith is the substance of things hoped for, the evidence of things not seen. Hebrews 11:1

As we talked about earlier, the three Hebrew boys had tremendous faith in God. They believed God could deliver them out of their circumstances. They didn't say God would deliver. They said God <u>could</u> deliver them from Neb-u-chad-nez'zer. They knew even if God didn't deliver them out of the fiery furnace, he would keep their minds in perfect peace.

God is able to deliver you at anytime from any situation. The problem many Christians face today, is they keep trying to keep God in a <u>BOX.</u> Why are you limiting what God can do in your life? He is an all-powerful God. There is nothing to hard for him. Just as he said, Let there be light, and there was light. God speaks your blessings into existence.

Some have great testimonies of how God has healed Poverty, Sterility, Cancer, Diabetes, Drugs, Prostitution, Alcohol's, etc. However, they won't believe God can heal them from their childhood traumas. If this is you? You are stuck at an impasse (limited faith). Impasse is when you are stuck, because you don't want to come out of your comfort zone. Therefore, you won't step up on your faith. You believe God can restore your finances, but not save your household. You believe God can give you a promotion, but not keep your body under subjection. The devil is a Liar!

Folks we do not have a limited God. The God we serve is the King of Kings and the Lord of Lords! He is the Alpha and Omega. He is the reason for our existence. He created the heavens and the earth. There was nothing before him and there can be nothing without him. Jesus is the foundation of my life. He is the rock that keeps me anchored! He is the sword that fights the good fight of faith. He is my shield in times of trouble.

"I can do all things through Christ which strengthenth me." Philippines 4:13. In order to make this walk this long, I had to grab hold of faith. I had to believe I can do all things through Jesus Christ, the author and finisher of my faith. I had to tell myself, when I felt myself slipping, God can keep my body under subjection; as long as I continue to submit unto him. God will strengthen my mind, spirit and soul. He has kept me through the storms, earthquakes, floods, and fires. During the fires, the Lord supplied me with water. Although I can not see the water. I will keep my eyes fasten upon the Lord. For I, know in the time

of trouble he shall hide me in the secret of his tabernacle.

There were times when I felt the fiery trails would over take me. However, when I looked closely into the fire, I'd see my deliver, Jesus. Jesus, had never left me. In my panic, I forgot to look up for direction.

I will lift up mine eyes unto the hills from whence cometh my help. (Psalms 121:1) God is our refuge and strength, a very present help in trouble. (Psalms 46:1) Our help is in the name of the Lord, who made heaven and earth. (Psalms 124:8)

God is the water needed to control and put the fire out. In order to learn to maintain until the fire is out, you must learn fire prevention methods. If you are going to keep yourself a clean vessel unto God, then you need to govern your life with things pleasing unto him. Let us examine some fire hazards of the flesh. Three of the top fire hazards to single christians are Ungodly music, Inappropriate television shows, and Unconcerned dating.

Music of today is filled with promoting sex, profanity, violence, and drugs. There is no edification to God in music depicting women as female dogs. There is no spiritual food for your spirit to be strengthen through this filth. This type of music feeds the frenzy of the flesh. It causes the flesh to rise and war against the spirit. The flesh wants immediate gratification. Listening to violent artist, is corrupting your mind, heart, and soul. *1 Corinthians 15:3, "Be not deceived: evil communication corrupts good manners."* Don't be deceived, you will begin to experience feelings from your flesh, that your heart and mind will want to react upon. You are not as strong as you think. I am not speaking from thought, but experience. We all thought we could listen to a little R&B or Jazz. However, it feeds the soul. The music puts you in certain moods. None of the moods are righteous or edifying to the Lord. And we cannot say, Lord we did not know you did not approve, because his word states:

Know ye not that the unrighteous shall not inherit the kingdom of God? Be not deceived: neither fornicators, not idolater, nor adulters, nor effeminate, nor abusers of themselves with mankind. Nor thieves, nor covetous, nor drunkards, nor revilers, nor extortioners: shall inherit the kingdom of God.

(I Corinthians 6:9-10)

Music is one of Americans favorite pass times, however the other is television. Most of Americans spend at least 20+ hours a week in front of the television set. Television has

40

become America's favorite recreational time. I am not against television. However, the majority of shows that are produced on most networks are full of sex, profanity, and violence. Majority of talk shows are degrading. People are coming on national television and talking about intimate parts of their lives. They are proud that they slept with more than one individual. You have show titles such as; " Women who love to love other women's men. I am really a woman, not a man. Men who love to cheat. My mother is dating my boyfriend." What kind of sin sick society enjoys watching others suffer emotional pain. The devil's society is my answer! The devil is loose and controlling America. America use to be a place where we stood by the statement on our money, "In God We Trust." Today, if you mention God in public or schools, we make a commotion.   Come on open your eyes.   Don't you think it's ludicrous, that this country banned prayer in schools, but find it morally correct to pass condoms out in schools.   The devil and his demons are on the rampage.   How could prayer compare to the mess of allowing underage girls to get abortions without parental consent.

Television, which I will rename to Hell-a-vision, is trying to make society accept immoral behavior.   If you are <u>not</u> having multiple sex partners, drinking alcohol, partying, or scheming on someone, then today's society considers <u>us</u> <u>abnormal</u>!

You read right.   I said, " Society considers Us abnormal."   I included myself in the abnormal category of today's societal values, because I don't buy into the devil's garbage.

On a daily basis, I ask God to crucify my flesh that I may be pleasing unto him.

Television has taken what God deems holy and made it unholy. Families that use to pray together are in different rooms watching obscenity. Singles are locked in their rooms watching men and women fornicating. However, Hell-a-vision isn't calling it fornication. They call it, love in the afternoon or late night adult television.

Turn off the Hell-a-vision, and have devotion. Sing, pray, and read the word. Some of the best times of my life is spent singing to God. I usually find a song that I can just romance God with. I sing about his goodness. How he gave me a second chance. How he has changed my life complete. Then, I talk to him about my day, desires, and disappointments. The Hell-a-vision can't help me to stand against the whiles of the devil. Hell-a-vision can't prepare me to be a good, loving, supporting wife. If your desire is to be married, then spend more time with God.

I had found in watching soap operas and certain sitcoms, my views of a relationships had become distorted. Hell-a-vision, made relationships look non-romantic, too dramatic, too sexual, and too many mind games. What I didn't remember was this was simply a factious script written to draw viewers. These relationships did not depict real life. It is not necessary to have drama every second. Every man is not cheating. Every woman is not scheming. Too much hell-television had sent my vision of love, dedication, straight to a vision of destruction and torment. I believed all men were not worthy of the ground women walked on. However, through guidance and direction of the Holy Ghost and my leaders, I know God does have a saved, sanctified, holy ghost filled man for me to call my husband. Therefore, if you are seeking a wife, then consult God. If you are waiting on a husband, wait patiently on the Lord. For the bible lets us know , *"Whoso findeth a wife findeth a good thing, and obtaineth favour of the Lord." Proverbs 18:22*

Remember to watch sensible television not hell-a-vision. For: *"The light of the body is the eye: therefore, when thine eye is single, thy whole body is full of light; but when thine eye is evil, thy body is full of darkness. Take heed therefore that the light which is in thee be not darkness. (Luke 11:34-35)*

Television and music usually tries to dictate how we should date. However, as Christians we are obligated not to let our good to be evil spoken of. Dating isn't evil, but the manner in which you date will be judge by sinners. If they see us in compromising situations, then they will believe you are sexually active with the individual. Here are just a few tips I remind myself with:

Remember, first and foremost I am human; and my flesh will rise to the appropriate occasion. Therefore, use wisdom and plan appropriately for the evening.

1. A restaurant, café, concert, play, family dinner, or church service. It is kind of hard to be caught in a compromising position in public.
2. Group date when I feel vulnerable. A little help goes a long way.
3. Don't date anyone who is not a believer of God's word. He\She will not respect the principles and practices I believe.

4. Look good, but not provocative. It is a date, not my honeymoon.

5. Don't think you have everything under control and go to an empty apartment. Because the night time is usually the right time for lust. Yes, I said lust, not love. Love is patient and kind. Lust usually doesn't care about consequences.

Watch and pray, that ye enter not into temptation: the spirit indeed is willing, but the flesh is weak. (Matthew 26:41)

Learn to pray and crucify the flesh on a daily basis.

Heavenly father, In the Name of Jesus:

I praise you for being a God of a second chance. I thank God for his redeeming power. Lord, I come to you humbly as I know. Please forgive me for my sins. I desire to be who you

47

would have me to be.   Help me Lord stand. Help me to stand against temptation.   Help me not to flirt with dangerous situations.   Lord, renew the right spirit in me.

Satan, I rebuke the demon of lust, and fornication, from my heart and mind! I rebuke the demonic forces that plague my heart and mind! I rebuke the demon of lust back into the pit of hell from whence it came.   My mind, spirit, and soul belong to the Lord. I will be Holy and acceptable unto God, which is my reasonable service. I am putting on the whole armor of God, to help me fight against the whiles of the devil. I will keep my conversation pleasing unto the Lord. I will continue to watch and pray not to enter into temptation.

Finally, my brethren, be strong in the Lord, and in the power of his might. Put on the whole armor of God, that ye may be able to stand against the wile of the devil. For we wrestle not against flesh and blood, but against the rulers of the darkness of this world, against spiritual wickedness in high places. Wherefore, take unto you the whole armor of God, that ye may be able to withstand in the evil day, and having done all, to stand. Stand therefore, having your loins girt with truth, and having on the breastplate of righteousness, And your feet shod with the preparation of the gospel of peace; Above all, taking the shield of faith, wherewith ye shall be able to quench all the fiery darts of the wicked. And take the helmet of salvation, and the sword of the Spirit, which is the word of God. (Ephesians 6:10-17)

CHAPTER FOUR

WAITING FOR THE SMOKE TO CLEAR

Wait on the Lord: be of good courage, and he shall strengthen thine heart: wait, I say, on the Lord. (Psalms 27:14)

After a fire is put out, the people usually stand around waiting for instructions. The victims want to know if they can go back into their homes, or should they make other arrangements. In any event, they have to wait for the Fire Chief instructions.

As Christians we must patiently wait for the Lords instructions in the mist of a test. It may seem as thou the worst of the storm is over. But, if you don't wait on how to proceed, then you could be exposing yourself to danger!

There are lessons to be learned in every test. During a test, if your responses are incorrect then you fail. When you fail, you have to learn the material and take the test again. (For best results follow the instructions in the word of God)

Waiting for an answer is the hardest test for most Christian singles. If God says yes or no, then we know how to proceed. When God says nothing, then we have a problem. We have a problem because we are not waiting patiently. I am not very patient when it came to standing on long lines. I refuse to go to certain stores because of the crowds. Why do I hate standing on long lines? Because there is simple nothing to do, but stand. You get tired of looking at your items. You get tired of looking at the person in front of you. You get tired of listening to everyone on line complain. I understand, why Jesus said, " Occupy until I come." We have to be busy for the kingdom of God.

I am sure many of you have gone through this situation. Well, while I was going through these years of test, people would ask me, why I wasn't married yet. I would say, "I am waiting on God to Bless me with a husband." The truth of the matter was, God was waiting for me to recognize him in all his glory. He was waiting for me to begin to work happily without a husband in the kingdom. That is when I opened my eyes and saw the many opportunities that were always before me, waiting for me to work consistently in the kingdom of God. Example: the usher board, choir, finance committee, secretary, nursing home outreach, youth leader, and Pulpit committee. *Whatsoever thy hands findeth to do.*

Do it with thy might...(Ecc 9:10) When you take care of Gods business, he takes care of your business. ·If you are busy working for the kingdom, you don't have time for a pity party. Pity parties are when you isolate yourself from others; to indulge in self charity.

When you entertain destructive behavior you drain yourself and dry up like a chip. You are too blessed. Lay to rest those dead issues that keep you returning back to your old ways. Stop Playing With Dead Things! Place your situation in God's hands. He knows your every desire. This is only a test! Jesus has a compassionate heart and holds our cares in his hands. Hold on. Be encouraged. God sees you. He knows your every desire. This is only a trial!. Jesus has you in his hands.

The word is a lamp unto my feet, and a light unto my path. (psalms 119:105)

God word is a lamp unto your feet. He will light your pathway as you go through this journey of life. Therefore, if you are looking to be a strong soldier in the Lord, then you have to go through basic training. Each training course has many obstacles. When you succeed by mastering every obstacle, then you will have a powerful testimony. Your testimony will encourage your heart every time a difficult course is before you. You will remember your foundation, which is Christ Jesus. It may seem as thou God has left you in the dark. But there is no darkness with God. There is only hope our greatest light.

This I recall to my mind, therefore, have I hope. It is of the Lords mercies that we are not consumed, because his compassion fail not. They are new mercies every morning: great is thy faithfulness. The Lord is my portion, saith my soul; therefore, will I hope I him. The Lord

55

is good unto them that wait for him, to the soul that seeketh him. The Lord is good unto them that wait for him, to the soul that seeketh him. It is good that a man should both hope an quietly wait for the salvation of the Lord.

(Lamentations 3:21-26)

When I am waiting for the smoke to clear I remind myself this too will pass. I keep a song in my heart and a praise in my mouth. Every morning remind yourself, great is Gods' faithfulness. God is not a God who can lie. When God promises to deliver you from a situation, then he will deliver. We are not fighting for the victory, but from the victory. Satan has no rule on your life. God is in control. Put your trust in him.

If you put your trust in God then you will not complain or murmur. If your faith and hope rest upon God then you will wait quietly and patiently. God will instruct you, if you

56

would shut up. No one can listen effectively if they are talking. Don't magnify your problem by talking about it constantly. Tell the Lord, from your heart, praise him for the deliverance, and let it go.

Remember if you don't open your mouth and let the devil know what your weaknesses are, then he has nothing to work with. He can only work with what you give him. He can't read your mind or your heart. He is not omnipotent, omnipresence, nor omniscience. He is waiting for you to let him know what is troubling you, and then magnify it. But we curse Satan through the Blood of Jesus. We will be more than conquerors. We will learn to hope and quietly wait for the change.

But they that wait upon the Lord shall renew their strength: they shall mount up with wings as eagles, they shall run, and not be weary, and they shall walk and not faint. (Isaiah 40:31)

Heavenly Father, in the name of Jesus:

We give all honor and glory unto. We thank you for being there in the times of trouble. We thank you for you love, mercy and understanding. Lord, we ask that you teach us to wait patiently upon you. That we walk in your will and direction we desire to MOUNT UP WITH AS EAGLES. We want to run this race and not get weary. We want to walk in love and not faint. Let us continue to pray for one another. Lifting up all saints that we maybe an encouragement to one another. Lord we ask you to guide us and keep us. We love you Jesus. We thank you for hearing our prayers. We recognize we can't mount up without you. We give your name the Praise,

Honor, and Glory. In Jesus name we pray. Amen.

CHAPTER FIVE

TIME TO REBUILD

When thou passest through the water, I will be with thee, and through the rivers, they shall not overflow thee. When thou walkest through the fire thou shalt not be burned; neither shall the flame kindle upon thee. (Isaiah 43:2)

Victory is already yours! When you pass through the storms, God will be with thee. When trails come as rivers, they shall not overflow thee. When fiery trails come upon you, thou shalt not be burned; neither shall the flame kindly upon thee. God has promised to be with you through every crisis. God's love and protection is the greatest security plan. There is no crisis that he can't handle. He is the all time crisis intervention counselor. When

61

God says he has your back, he has your back! You can comfortably lean back knowing the Lord is there to help hold you up. Therefore, when God is holding you up, you need to give him the praise. Through my most difficult times I found that deliverance was in the Praise.

God, my heart is fixed; I will sing and give praise, even with my glory. Awake, psaltery and harp. I myself will awake early. I will praise thee, O Lord, among the people and I will sing praises unto thee among the nations. For thy mercy is great above the heaven: and thy truth readeth unto the clouds. (Psalm 108:1-4)

Our God loves to hear your praises. Praise him when you are happy, sad, sick, confused, lonely, depressed, lied on, used, abused, and refused. Jesus has been merciful unto you. You know he has redeemed you(just as he did me) from things man, and woman would condemn. Jesus picked you up all dirty, smelling, and drowning in your own blood. He looked past you sins and accepted you into the royal family. Jesus is worthy to be praised! He sacrificed his life, for the remission of our sins. He is the only one who can have agape love. Praise Jesus for his goodness. Praise him for his mercy. Praise him for the warm blood running through your veins. Praise him for your home, family, job, school, car, finances, health, salvation, redemption, the Holy Ghost, the word, and etc, etc, etc, and etc.

If you take a journey back you will praise Jesus' Holy name. He has showed us by his example, the meaning of Love. Jesus loves us inspite of who we were or what we had done. I praise the Lord for his mercy and grace.

In Psalms, David said, " I will bless the Lord at all times: His praises shall continually be in my mouth." (Psalms 34:1) Many are the afflictions of the righteous: but the Lord delivereth him out of the all (Psalms 34:19) Thou David had trails and tribulations he yet praised the Lord. When he fought Goliath, he gave God the praise. When Saul sought his life, he yet gave God the Praise. When his kingdom was overthrown, he yet gave God the Praise. Upon his dying bed, he yet gave God the Praise.

Beloved, think it not strange concerning the fiery trail which is to try you, as though some strange thing happened unto you: But rejoice, inasmuch as ye are partaker of Christ sufferings; that when his glory shall be revealed, ye maybe glad also with exceeding joy. (I Peter 4:12)

Think it not strange when situations come upon you. The Lord has already told you that fiery trails will try you. He also stated to rejoice as partakers of Christ sufferings. I don't believe anyone has or will suffer more than Jesus did. From birth Herod sought to take his life. The Pharisees and Saducees sought to kill him. His family didn't seem to understand his purpose. His disciples doubted him, cursed him and sold him. He was stripped naked and humiliated. Then whipped and spat on. He was crucified for our transgressions. Jesus was single, but not alone. When Satan tempted him, he stood on the word. Jesus always asked his Father for what he needed. As singles we are to do the very same today. We are to pray for guidance and direction. We are to dedicate our time to the Lord. Make the Lord the lover of your life. Loneliness will soon leave and joy will return. When we connect with God on a daily basis, then we open the doors of wonderful possibilities to minister to the sick, and broken hearted.

Practice reading and studying your word. The word is your road map to receiving all the desires of your heart. And as Apostle Paul so wonderfully said," Wherefore I desire that ye faint not at my tribulations for you, which is your glory. For this cause I bow my knees unto the Father of our Lord Jesus Christ. Of whom the whole family in heaven and earth is named, That he would grant you, according to the riches of his glory, to be strengthened with might by his Spirit in the inner man; That Christ may dwell in your hearts by faith; that ye being rooted and grounded in love, May be able to comprehend with all saints what is the breadth, and length, and depth, and height; And to know the love of Christ, which passeth knowledge that you might be filled with all the fullness of God. Now unto him that is able to do exceeding abundantly above all that we ask or think, according to the power that worketh in us, Unto him be glory in the church by Christ

Jesus throughout all ages, world without end Amen. ❤ (Ephesians 3:13-21)

CHAPTER SIX

BRUSH FIRES

Brush fires are fires that occur for brief encounters at a time. However, don't take them lightly, they are little fires that if not extinguished immediately will spread quickly. We usually here about brush fires in very dry and warm places.

"When the unclean spirit is gone out of a man, he walketh through dry places, seeking rest, and findeth none. Then he saith, I will return into my house from whence I came out; and when he is come, he findeth it empty, swept, and garnished. Matt. 12:43-44

Satan never gives up fight to rob, kill, and destroy you. He will keep sending his demons of loneliness, lust, and depression to you.

However, if you are prayed up and working daily in the kingdom of God, you will have a better chance of detecting when a brush fire is breaking out.

Why can't we detect brush fires? The problem is far too often we become on fire for the Lord in intervals. For weeks or months we are running strong for the Lord. We attend church services, on a regular basis. We attend choir rehearsals, the usher board, missionary, deacon, evangelist or ministers board meetings. We testify about the goodness of God to everyone. However, because we have not truly given the desire of a mate over to the Lord, we begin to fade again. This is when a demon will show up. He tells you, "See you have been dedicated to Lord and you are still alone. There are no suspects or prospects. You have been obedient to your leader and nothing. You have been holy and acceptable unto the Lord and nothing. You have prayed and fasted and nothing. I think He forgot about you. You see the other sisters and brothers have somebody. You think, you know what they are doing? They weren't doing all you were doing. All this is so unfair!"

The devil is a LIAR! Unfortunately, we lend our ears to these demons. We listen until we almost get knocked off of our feet.

"I had fainted, unless I had believed to see the goodness of the Lord in the land of the living." Psalms 27: 13

After we have fainted in our minds and almost in our physical bodies, we remember the promises of God. Jesus said, "He will never leave us nor forsake us." The word also let us know, there is no good thing He will withhold from us. Then through the power of the Holy Ghost we rebuke the enemy.

If the approach above is the one you have been taken over and over again, this is the wrong defense. Instead of waiting until you faint, immediately rebuke your mind, body, and soul.

Pray In The Time of Trouble.

Heavenly Father in the Name of your son Jesus, I need your help NOW! I feel the enemy attacking my flesh. In James 4:7, you told me to submit myself to you. Resist the devil, and he will flee from me. I am therefore, submitting myself, as humbly as I know how. Please let your angels encamp round about me. (Now address your enemy) Satan, you are a liar. I have been delivered from loneliness, depression, fornication, masturbation, and any other sexual thoughts. (Lay hands on yourself) devil you can't have my mind. I am a child of the King. I am holy and acceptable unto the Lord, this is my reasonable service. If the Lord endured the cross, then I can endure celibacy. I can bring my flesh under subjection. I can maintain until my change comes. My God is an all sufficient God. When I am weak, he is strong. Therefore, by the power and might of the Holy Ghost, I am Holy for God is Holy. Remind yourself daily that God is to be Glorified in the body.

Know ye not that the unrighteous shall not inherit the kingdom of God? Be not deceived: neither fornicators, nor idolaters, nor adulterers, nor effeminate, nor abusers of themselves with mankind, Nor thieves, nor covetous, nor drunkards, nor revilers, nor extortioners, shall inherit the kingdom of God. (1Corinthians 6:9-10)

These scriptures may sound harsh, but scriptures like these will help you jump up on your feet quickly. When you arm yourself with the word of God, then you have the best defense strategy. You will not have time to slip and slide in the mud. You will recognize your short coming and get up, repent, and praise God for the victory.

People, usually ask me how am I making it, because they are barely hanging on. I tell them, there were times when I was hanging on. However, I am currently holding on to the promises of God.

The difference between hanging on and holding on:

1. Hanging on implies you are about to fall, unless help is dispatched immediately. Words associated with the word hanging are: suspended, dangling, swinging, and pendulant.

2. Holding on means you have some form of control over the situation. Words associated with holding are: Keeping, gripping, retaining, maintaining, and containing.

On a daily basis, I arm myself for spiritual warfare. I remind myself that it is Satan's job to get me to fall. I equip my mind with the consequences of being disobedient to God. The fact that, no man knows the day nor the hour that the son of man will return, keeps me level headed. There is nothing or no one worth my salvation. There is nothing or no one worth your salvation. Don't be like the 5 foolish virgins. Remember they did not prepare for when the bridegroom appeared. Will you be ready? Are you ready if Jesus returns tonight? If not, then repent and re-claim your life to

Jesus. Sex, money, music or friendship isn't worth being separated from the Love of God.

For I am persuaded, that neither death, not life, not angels, nor principalities, nor powers, nor things present, nor things to come, nor height nor depth, nor any other creature shall be able to separate us from the love of god, which is in Christ Jesus our Lord.   (KJV) Romans 8:38-39

God has some awesome rewards for obedience. When you walk uprights before the Lord, he will give you the desires of your heart. He said, there is nothing I can't ask of him and he won't do it. Therefore, in his appointed time he will provide me with husband that will love, honor, and cherish me until death due us part. Anything God puts together will avail. Anything we put together without God, is simply a game of Russian roulette. There are many emotionally disturb individuals in this world. Men and women are being raped, beaten, and killed everyday by their partners or spouse. Listen, no relationship is worth your life! Therefore, get wisdom with a good understanding of WHO you are and WHOSE you are.

Happy is the man that findeth wisdom, and the man that getteth understanding. Proverbs 1:13

For wisdom is better than rubies; and all the things that may be desired are not to be compared to it. Proverbs 8:11

CHAPTER SEVEN

FIRE PREVENTION

There are five steps, I want to share with you for preventing the fire from reoccurring.

1. Put on the whole armor of God.
2. Fast and Pray.
3. Study the Bible.
4. Participate in Church Services regularly.
5. Keep Your Mind on Things of God.

1. Put On The Whole Armour Of God-Ephesians 6:10-17

Finally, my brethen be strong in the Lord, and in the power of his might. Put on the whole armour of God, that ye may be able to stand against the wiles of the devil. For we wrestle not against flesh and blood, but against principlaities, against powers, against the rulers of the darkness of this world, against spiritual wickedness n high places. Wherefore, take unto you the whole armour of God, that ye may be able to withstand in the evil day, and having done all to stand. Stand therefore, having your loins girt about with truth, and having on the breastplate of righteousness; And your feet shod with the preparation of the gospel of peace; Above all, taking the shield of faith, wherewith ye shall be able to quench all the fiery darts of the wicked. And take the helmet of salvation, and the sword of the Spirit, which is the word of God.

You know that the enemy will fight your flesh daily. He will bring all types of thoughts to your mind. Therefore, it is essential that you are equip on a daily basis, for this attack. Pray every morning while putting on your armour.

Your armour is your fighting gear. Every good soldier is prepared for war. Be Prepared Daily.

2. Fast and Pray - Matthew 17:21

And Jesus said unto them, Because of your unbelief: for verily I say unto you, If ye have faith as a grain of mustard seed, ye shall say unto this mountain, Remove hence to yonder place; and it shall remove; and nothing shall be impossible unto you. Howbeit this kind goeth not out but by prayer and fasting.

3. Study the Bible - 2 Timothy 2:15

Study to shew thyself approved unto God, a workman that needeth not to be ashamed, rightly dividing the word of truth.

4. Participate In Church Services Regularly - Hebrew 10:25

Not forsaking the assembling of ourselves together, as the manner of some is; but exhorting one another: and so much the more, as ye see the day approaching.

5. Keep Your Mind on Things of God - Philippians 4:7-8

And the peace of God, which passeth all understanding, shall keep your hears and minds through Christ Jesus. Finally, brethren, whatsoever things are true, whatsoever things are honest, whatsoever thing are just, whatsoever things are pure, whatsoever things are lovely, whatsoever things are of good report; if there be any virtue, and if there be any praise, think on these things.

Daily Journal Prescreening- we have talked about walking through the flames an not getting burnt. Some of you are already in the flames. Some of you have already been burnt. Therefore, you need a change. You need a change in behavior, and circumstances. Many of problems come from our own desires. We want what we want, when we want it. God doesn't work in our time. He works in his own time.

Keep this journal for a month. Answer the questions first to determine where you need to start. The Journal is to help you see where you are in self, and where you would like to go in God. This won't work unless you are truthful with yourself.

DAILY JOURNAL

- **Write down the current desires of your heart**--

----------------.

- **Write down the plans you have to achieve these desires**

_____

_____

_____

_____

_____

_____

_____

_____

_____

_____

_____

_____

_____

- **Compare the two lists to what God says in his word for his children. Is there a conflict? (i.e. Are you unequally yoked with an unbeliever, because you want to get married? Are you forsaken attending church for your own personal gain of wealth? Are you patiently waiting on the Lord or are you trying to help?)**

_____

_____

_____

_____

_____

_____

_____

_____

_____

_____

_____

_____

- **I have examined myself and recognize, I need the Lord to work out the following situations in me. God Help Me with**

_____

_____

_____

_____

_____

_____

_____

_____

_____

_____

_____

_____

_____

_____

Many times the activities we are involved in hinder us.

- **Write down the television shows you watch regularly**

_____

_____

_____

_____

_____

_____

_____

_____

_____

- **Is there sex and violence in these shows?**

_____

_____

_____

_____

_____

_____

_____

_____

- **How long do you spend watching these types of shows?**

_____

_____

_____

_____

_____

_____

_____

_____

_____

Other times it is the people we let influence our lives.

- Write down your friends and if they are believers Christ.

_____

_____

_____

_____

_____

_____

_____

_____

_____

_____

_____

_____

_____

_____

_____

_____

- **Are they single, married, divorced?**

_____

_____

_____

_____

_____

_____

_____

_____

- Do they encourage you through the word of God? _____

- Write the days you are dedicating to fast for a change.

_____

_____

_____

_____

_____

_____

_____

_____

_____

Encouragement for your Change

Philippians 4:13 - I can do all things through Christ which strengtheneth me.

If your are serious and ready to begin your change, then begin. Tell, Our Father that today _____, I commit the following situations unto him.

1. _____

_____

2. _____

_____

3. _____

_____

4. _____

_____

5. _____

_____

6. _____

_____

7. _____

_____

ENCOURAGE YOURSELF DAILY THROUGH AFFIRMATIONS OF GOD.

I believe God for my change. I believe God for a fresh annointing. I believe God for my husband/wife. I believe God for my family to get saved. I believe God for my ministry, health, etc....... I BELIEVE GOD! I BELIEVE GOD! I BELIEVE GOD!

ENCOURAGE YOURSELF DAILY THROUGH THE WORD!

Daily pick a scripture of encouragement. Reflect on it throughout the day. At the end write the scripture in your journal and the encouragement it gave you through the day.

ENCOURAGE YOURSELF THROUGH BOLD PRAYER.

Let us therefore come boldly unto the throne of grace, that we may obtain mercy, and find grace to help in time of need. Hebrews 4:16

ENCOURAGE FROM THE AUTHOR.

I believe through this book many strongholds will be broken. Take comfort in knowing that I am not speaking from past experience. I am saved, single and living for God. Focus on things you would like to achieve in life. Then set out to accomplish them. While you are single it is a great opportunity to advance in the ministry, your education, and employment. Your time should be wisely spent now. If you like to travel, get some Christian friends together and travel. Start a singles ministry in the church.

You should be clearing any financial debts. The worst thing to do is start a marriage with financial debt. Therefore, while you are single, consolidate bills, and invest in your future.

Regardless of what society states, you are not half of a whole. God created you in his image. And I think it is safe to say, God is not half of anything. Therefore, improve you and who God wants you to be. Then when your time comes, you are ready spiritually and naturally.

I pray earnestly that the Lord, will bless you as you embark on this wonderful transformation into his will and direction. I believe God will help you crucify your flesh on a daily basis. I believe God will give you the desires of your heart. You are more than a conqueror, and I am touching and agree that the Lord will led and direct you in the path of righteousness

Stay Encouraged for the Lord our God Loves you.

In Jesus Name, I pray

Amen.

About The Author

I am a single Christian woman. I attend Redeem Church of God and Prophecy in Brooklyn, NY. I am an Evangelist and youth pastor. I have my Ph.D. in Philosophy in Counseling Psychology. I have been saved and loving the Lord for ten years. I enjoy writing plays, poetry and inspirational books.

Printed in the United States
2318